D1709396

SCATALOG

A Kid's Field Guide to Animal Poop

HOW TO TRACK A DEER

Norman D. Graubart

"BECAUSE EVERYBODY POOPS"

WINDMILL BOOKS

New York

Published in 2015 by Windmill Books, an Imprint of Rosen Publishing
29 East 21st Street, New York, NY 10010

First Edition

Editor: Katie Kawa
Book Design: Michael J. Flynn

Photo Credits: Cover (deer), p. 6 (all) Tom Reichner/Shutterstock.com; cover (poop) Lost Mountain Studio/Shutterstock.com; back cover, pp. 1, 3–8, 10–20, 22–24 (deer hide) subin pumsom/Shutterstock.com; pp. 4, 21 Bruce MacQueen/Shutterstock.com; p. 5 marekuliasz/Shutterstock.com; p. 7 pavalena/Shutterstock.com; p. 8 Steve Byland/Shutterstock.com; p. 9 jcrader/iStock/Thinkstock.com; p. 10 Scott E Read/Shutterstock.com; p. 11 Nate Allred/Shutterstock.com; p. 12 graham tomlin/Shutterstock.com; p. 13 JR Trice/Shutterstock.com; p. 14 Ms.K/Shutterstock.com; p. 15 (top) cypriand/Shutterstock.com; pp. 15 (bottom), 16 (individual pellets), 22 (poop) Enrico Boscariol/E+/Getty Images; p. 16 (clumps of pellets) mb-fotos/iStock/Thinkstock.com; p. 16 (shiny poop) Tyler Olson/Shutterstock.com; p. 16 (dry poop) a40757/Shutterstock.com; p. 17 Aspen Photo/Shutterstock.com; p. 18 Stephen St. John/National Geographic/Getty Images; p. 19 Tom Edwards/Visuals Unlimited/Getty Images; p. 20 Igor/Normann/Shutterstock.com; p. 22 (deer) rSnapshotPhotos/Shutterstock.com.

Library of Congress Cataloging-in-Publication Data

Graubart, Norman D., author.
  How to track a deer / Norman D. Graubart.
      pages cm. — (Scatalog : a kid's field guide to animal poop)
  Includes index.
ISBN 978-1-4777-5416-0 (pbk.)
ISBN 978-1-4777-5417-7 (6 pack)
ISBN 978-1-4777-5415-3 (library binding)
1. Deer—Juvenile literature. 2. Animal droppings—Juvenile literature. 3. Animal tracks—Juvenile literature. 4. Tracking and trailing—Juvenile literature. I. Title.
QL737.U55G727 2015
599.65—dc23
                                    2014026050

Manufactured in the United States of America

CPSIA Compliance Information: Batch # CW15WM: For Further Information contact Rosen Publishing, New York, New York at 1-800-237-9932

CONTENTS

Deer in the Wild 4

North American Deer.. 6

Bucks, Does, and Fawns.............................. 8

What Hunts Deer? 10

Time to Eat!... 12

Deer Poop Differences 14

Tracking with Poop!.................................. 16

Other Ways to Track 18

Follow the Trail 20

Hunting and Helping 22

Glossary.. 23

Index 24

Websites 24

DEER IN THE WILD

Have you ever seen a deer? They're big, plant-eating **mammals** that walk on four legs. Different species, or kinds, of deer can be found throughout North America. Deer are a popular animal for people to hunt in the United States.

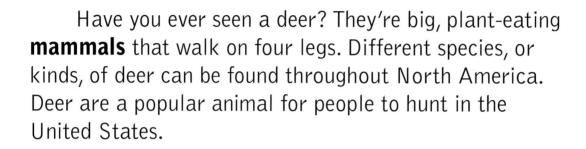

People hunt deer for sport and for their meat. Deer meat is called venison.

plant matter

pellet

Deer poop often looks like small ovals or circles. These are called pellets. You can often see seeds or other pieces of the plants deer eat in the pellets.

In order to find and track deer, hunters can follow their poop! Just looking at some deer poop can tell hunters a lot about whether or not they're in the right place. Tracking animals using poop is just one of many skills hunters master.

NORTH AMERICAN DEER

The two main kinds of deer in North America are the mule deer and the white-tailed deer. Mule deer live mostly in the mountains, deserts, and forests of western North America. They have large, pointy ears, as mules do. Their tails have a black tip. Mule deer are also slightly larger and heavier than white-tailed deer.

Male mule deer and white-tailed deer both have **antlers**. They lose their antlers during the winter and grow them back in the spring.

white-tailed deer

mule deer

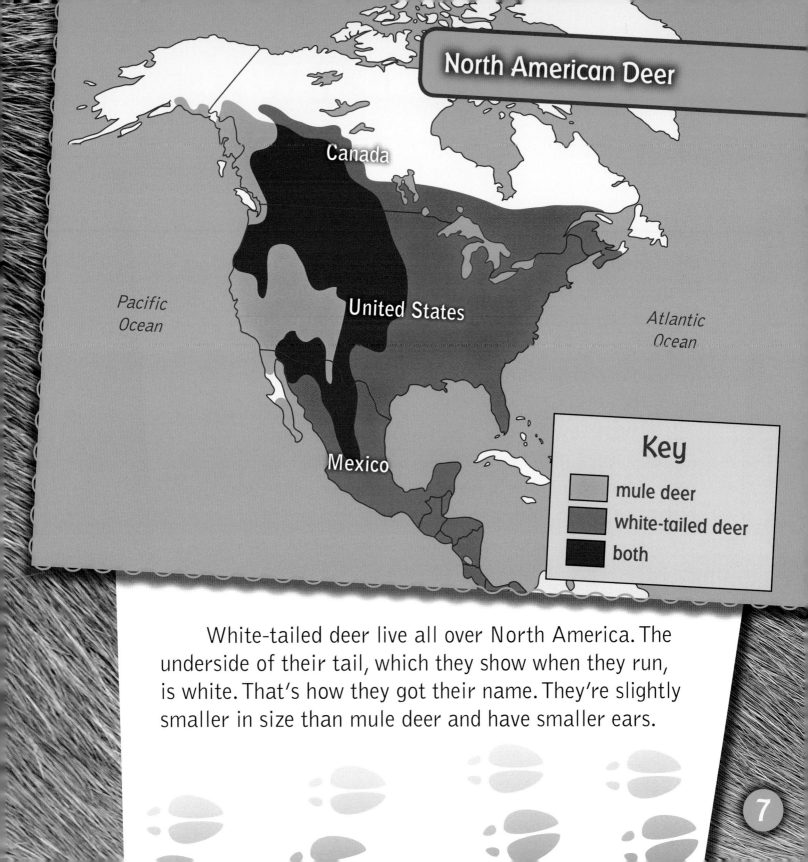

North American Deer

Canada

Pacific
Ocean

United States

Atlantic
Ocean

Mexico

Key

mule deer

white-tailed deer

both

White-tailed deer live all over North America. The underside of their tail, which they show when they run, is white. That's how they got their name. They're slightly smaller in size than mule deer and have smaller ears.

Both mule and white-tailed deer **mate** once a year. Male deer, called bucks, fight each other over the female deer, or does, they want to mate with. They do this by ramming their antlers against each other. After mating, fawns, or baby deer, are born in the spring. Deer often live in meadows and open fields during the summer. When the weather gets cold, they go into the forest.

Deer know how to **communicate** with one another. They get the attention of other deer by making certain noises. Fawns make noises, called bleats, that their mother can understand.

Fawns are born with special markings, such as spots, to help them hide from predators.

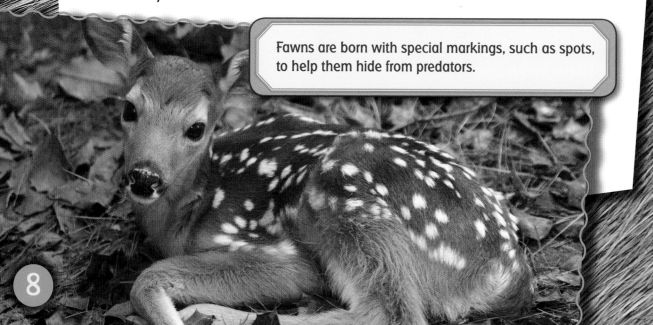

The size of the poop a fawn leaves behind is smaller than that of an adult deer. This is because fawns are smaller and eat less than adult deer.

Fawns begin to walk the same day they're born! Mother deer still take care of their babies, though. Mothers teach their fawns to find food and keep them safe from predators. Fawns stay with their mother for 1 to 2 years after they're born.

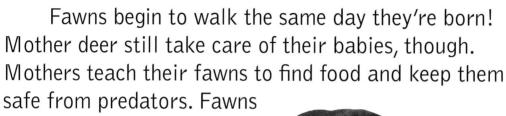

Predators, such as this cougar, track deer in order to eat them.

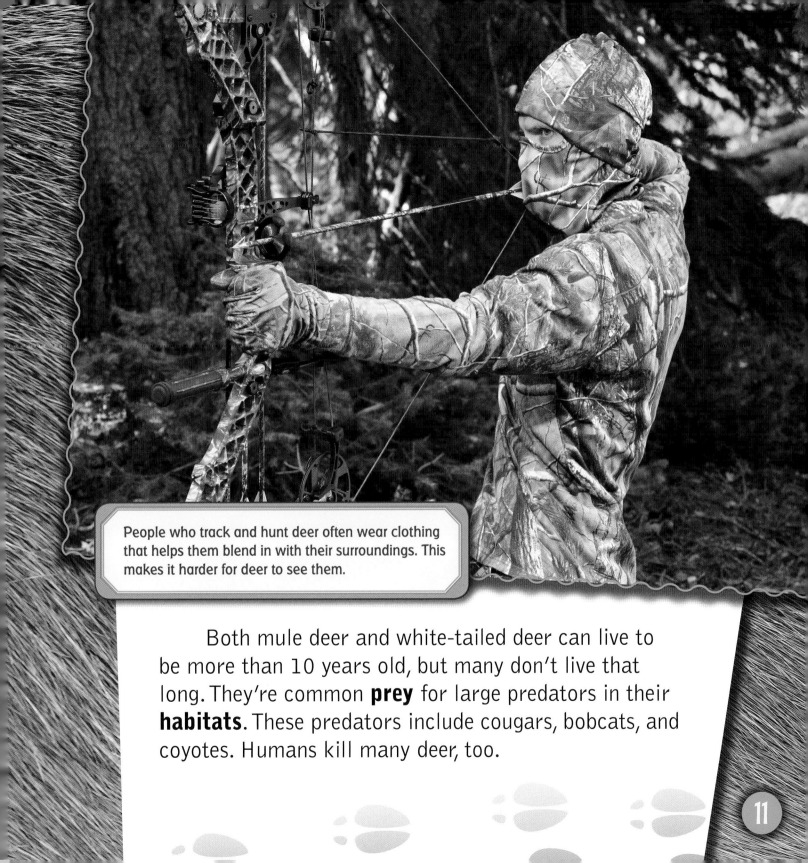

People who track and hunt deer often wear clothing that helps them blend in with their surroundings. This makes it harder for deer to see them.

Both mule deer and white-tailed deer can live to be more than 10 years old, but many don't live that long. They're common **prey** for large predators in their **habitats**. These predators include cougars, bobcats, and coyotes. Humans kill many deer, too.

TIME TO EAT!

Deer are herbivores, which means they only eat plants. They browse on a **variety** of plants depending on what's around them. It's easier for deer to find food in warmer weather. It's often harder to find food in the winter because of the cold, snowy weather.

Browsing means eating stems, leaves, and shoots, which are baby plants. The twigs and leaves eaten by deer are sometimes called browse, too.

WHITE-TAILED DEER DIGESTIVE SYSTEM

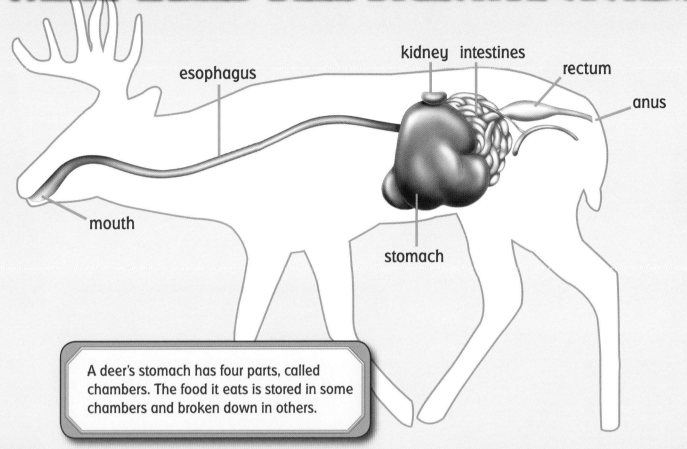

esophagus

kidney intestines

rectum

anus

mouth

stomach

A deer's stomach has four parts, called chambers. The food it eats is stored in some chambers and broken down in others.

White-tailed deer eat grass, fruits, seeds, twigs, and leaves during the summer. During the fall and winter, they eat nuts, dried leaves, and twigs. Mule deer eat leaves and grasses in the summer. When winter comes, they eat **shrubs**, twigs, and parts of conifers, which are trees that have cones and needles.

DEER POOP DIFFERENCES

The **process** of breaking down food into stuff an animal's body can use is called digestion. Poop is the leftover waste the body can't use after digestion takes place. Deer digest different food at different times of the year, so their poop looks different, too.

A deer's body is able to digest many different types of plants.

A deer's poop can tell us a lot about what it was eating!

Individual pellets of deer poop often come from a deer that has been eating leaves and twigs. If the pellets form big clumps, the deer was eating grasses and weeds. It's hard to tell just by looking at the poop whether it came from a doe or a buck.

TRACKING WITH POOP!

How can poop help people track deer? If the poop is shiny and brown, that means it's new. There should be a deer in the area. If it's dry or discolored, that means it's older. The deer that left this poop may not be in the area anymore.

WHAT DOES THE POOP TELL US?

○ **Individual Pellets:** The deer that left these had been eating drier plant parts, such as leaves or twigs.

○ **Shiny Poop:** This poop is new. The deer that left these can't be too far away.

○ **Clumps of Pellets:** The deer that left these had been eating grasses and weeds.

○ **Dry Poop:** This poop is old and hard. The deer that left these did so a long time ago.

Masking your scent with a deer's poop confuses the deer you're tracking. They think you're also a deer because you smell like one!

Deer poop can also help people track deer in other ways. Deer are less likely to smell a person in the area if they have some deer poop on their shoes. This is called masking your scent. Always ask an adult to help you do this safely.

You can find deer using more than just their poop. Have you ever seen deer tracks? Each deer hoof print has two long ovals that look somewhat like raindrops with two small circles or ovals at the bottom. The direction of the long shapes tells you which direction the deer was walking. Bigger prints mean bigger deer.

long ovals

2–4 inches (5–10 cm)

small circles

The size of a deer's hoof print depends on many things, including the size and age of the deer. Bucks also leave larger hoof prints than does.

18

Bucks also leave their scent behind when they rub their antlers against a tree.

If you're in a wooded area, look at the trees around you. You may find part of a tree trunk that's worn away. Bucks rub against trees to get rid of **velvet** covering their antlers. The worn part of the tree is called a deer rub.

FOLLOW THE TRAIL

Many animals track deer by following their scent. Some kinds of dogs are good at tracking deer by smelling them. Dachshunds, bloodhounds, and beagles are known for being good at tracking. People can track deer by using their own senses, too. For example, a hunter may hurt a deer without killing it. If it runs away, the hunter may be able to see a trail of blood. Following the trail may lead the hunter to the deer.

If you go hunting, make sure to follow all the hunting laws for your state, and always hunt with an adult.

Dogs can track deer better than people because they have a stronger sense of smell.

Hunting often takes place during certain seasons that are decided by each state. This keeps hunters from killing too many deer.

HUNTING AND HELPING

Deer have a lot of fawns, so they can take over neighborhoods. Deer hunting makes sure there are never too many deer in an area. People other than hunters track deer, too. Scientists track deer to study them. They help the government decide how to set hunting laws.

The next time you're in a forest or meadow, keep your eyes open for deer poop. It may look gross, but it's an important way to learn about these animals.

Learning how to track deer is important for hunters, but it's also important for people who want to study and **protect** deer, such as scientists.

GLOSSARY

antler (ANT-luhr) The solid, often branched horn of a deer.

communicate (kuh-MYOO-nuh-kayt) To share ideas and feelings.

habitat (HA-buh-tat) The natural home for plants, animals, and other living things.

mammal (MA-muhl) Any warm-blooded animal whose babies drink milk and whose body is covered with hair or fur.

mate (MAYT) To come together to make babies.

prey (PRAY) An animal hunted by other animals for food.

process (PRAH-sehs) A series of actions or changes.

protect (pruh-TEHKT) To keep safe.

shrub (SHRUHB) A woody plant that has several stems and is smaller than most trees.

variety (vuh-RY-uh-tee) A number or collection of different things.

velvet (VEHL-vuht) The soft skin covering the growing antler of a deer.

INDEX

A
antlers, 6, 8, 19

B
browse, 12
bucks, 8, 15, 18, 19

D
does, 8, 15, 18
dogs, 20
dry poop, 16

F
fawns, 8, 9, 10, 22

H
herbivores, 12
hoof prints, 18

M
mammals, 4
mule deer, 6, 7, 8, 11, 13

P
pellet clumps, 15, 16
pellets, 5, 15, 16
predators, 8, 10, 11

S
scent, 17, 19, 20
shiny poop, 16
species, 4

V
venison, 4

W
white-tailed deer, 6, 7, 8, 11, 13

WEBSITES

For web resources related to the subject of this book, go to:
www.windmillbooks.com/weblinks and select this book's title.